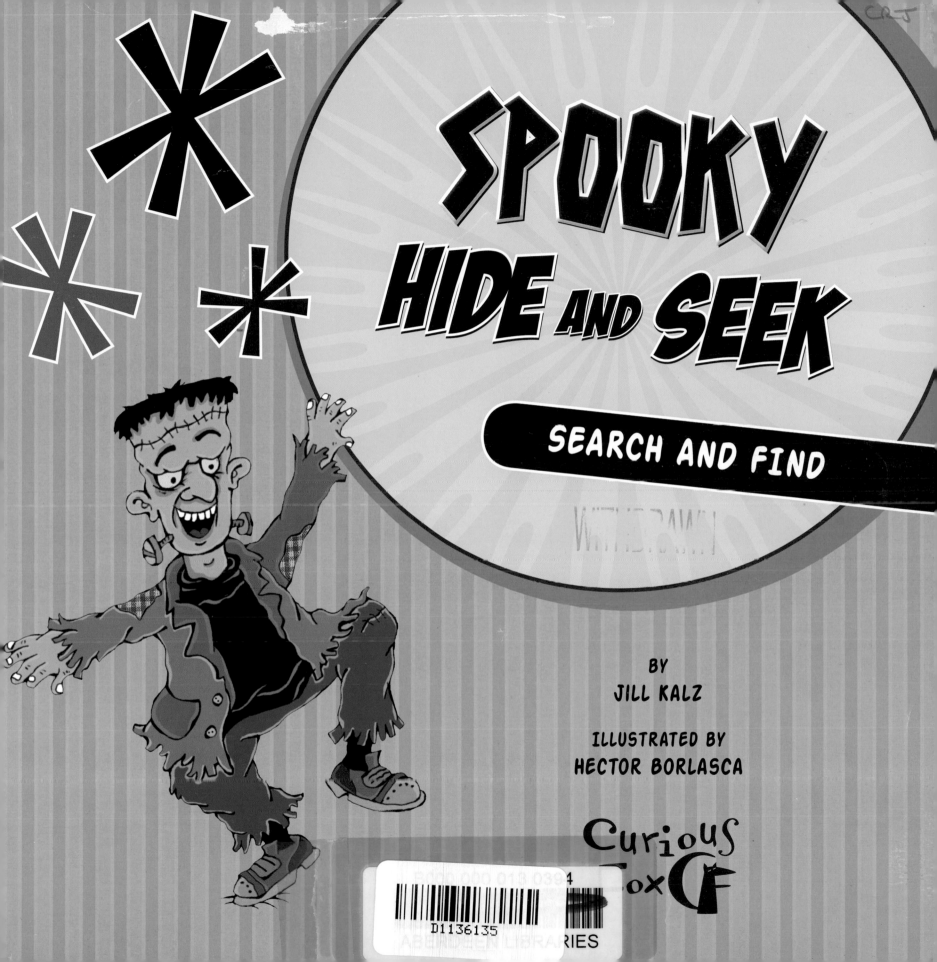

SPOOKY
HIDE AND SEEK

SEARCH AND FIND

BY
JILL KALZ

ILLUSTRATED BY
HECTOR BORLASCA

Curious
Fox

First published in 2014 by Curious Fox, an imprint of Capstone Global Library Limited, 7 Pilgrim Street, London, EC4V 6LB – Registered company number: 6695582

www.curious-fox.com

Designer: Lori Bye
Art Director: Nathan Gassman
Production Specialist: Danielle Ceminsky
The illustrations in this book were created digitally.

ISBN 978-1-78202-135-3
18 17 16 15 14
10 9 8 7 6 5 4 3 2 1

British Library Cataloguing in Publication Data
A full catalogue record for this book is available from the British Library.

Printed in China

WELCOME, SEARCHERS!

Look at the pictures and find the items on the lists. The first few puzzles are tricky. The next ones are even trickier. And the final puzzles are for the bravest seekers only. Good luck!

TABLE OF CONTENTS

Halloween Street

robot

cat

bat

squirrel

Frankenstein

witch

Haunted Hash and Monster Mash

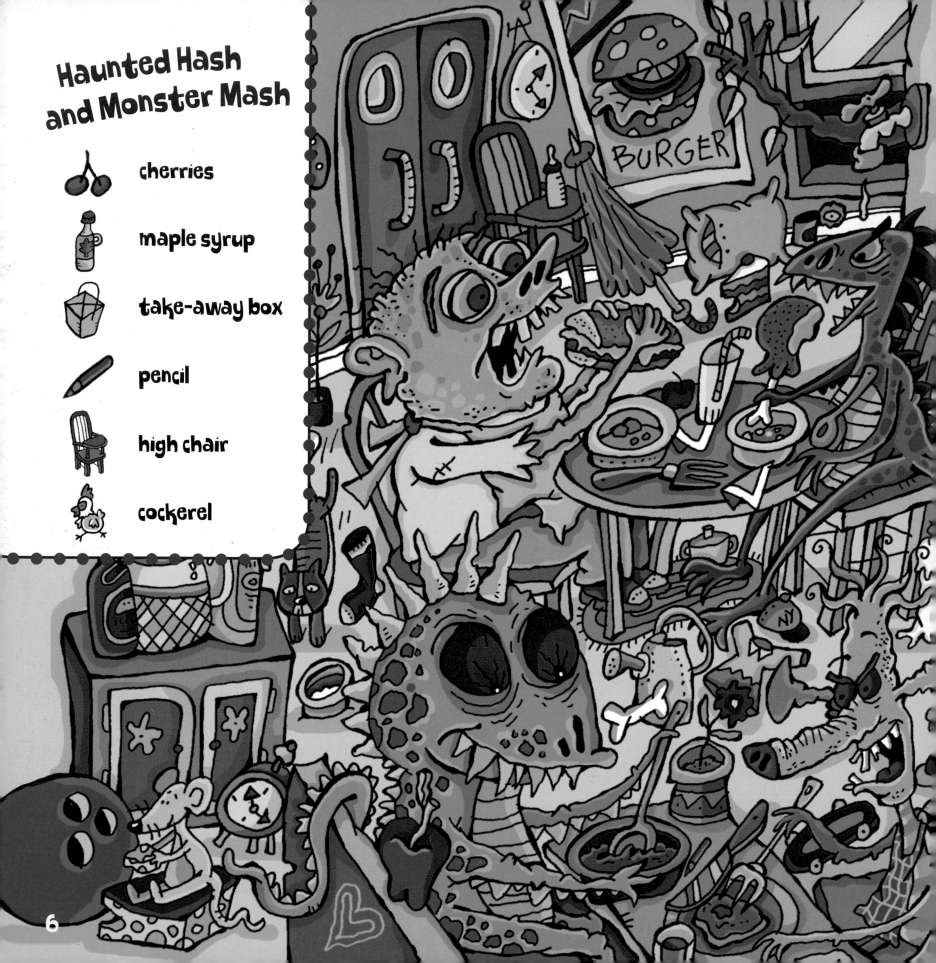

- cherries
- maple syrup
- take-away box
- pencil
- high chair
- cockerel

Spooky Lagoon

- treasure chest
- ship's wheel
- snorkel mask
- clown fish
- anchor
- sea horse

8

Gobs of Goodies

- toothbrush
- toothpaste
- pretzel
- hat
- pencil
- spider

Nightmares on Parade

- musical note
- crown
- pink sock
- sunglasses
- whistle
- lollipop

13

Monster Mansion

- scissors
- glasses
- moon
- snake
- star
- broom
- tombstone
- owl
- lock and key

15

Too Ghoul for School

 pumpkin

 crayons

 spider

 top hat

 milk

 class pet

 globe

 skipping rope

 pencil

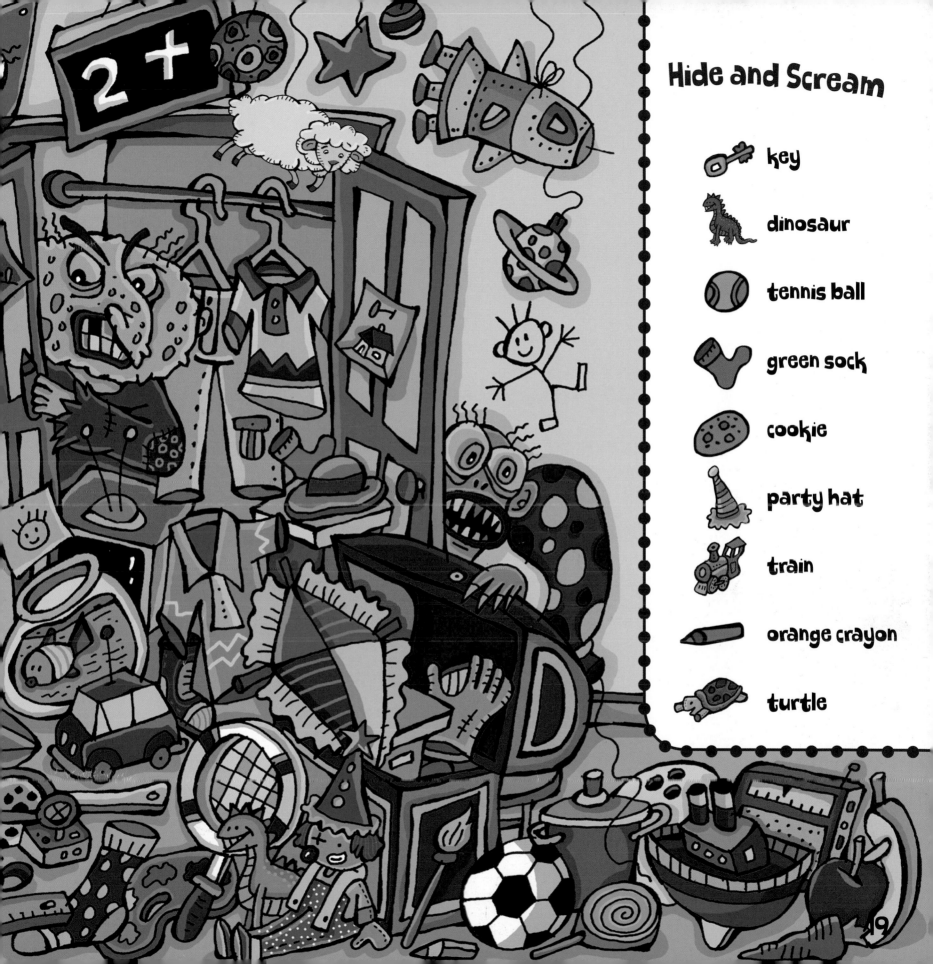

Hide and Scream

- key
- dinosaur
- tennis ball
- green sock
- cookie
- party hat
- train
- orange crayon
- turtle

Pumpkin Picking

- boot
- rat
- mittens
- witch's hat
- broom
- mummy
- fairy
- dog
- one-eyed jack-o'-lantern

The Witching Hour

- candle
- magic potion
- piece of cake
- raven
- skull
- jack-o'-lantern
- spider
- pocket watch
- cat

Campfire Fright

 RIP letters

 flashlight

 pumpkin

 canoe

 lantern

 guitar

 spider's web

 heart

 baseball cap

 human spray

tent

 teddy bear

24

A Wizard's World

 shoe

 cookie jar

 postcard

 chessboard

 snake

 unicorn

 dragon

 eyeball

 teapot

 wooden spoon

 garlic

 skull

Alien Attack

 doughnut

 mushroom

 sunglasses

 hot chocolate

 cap

 woodpecker

 slingshot

 camera

 boot

 rabbit

 melted snowman

 helmet

28

Tricks and Treats

 eye patch

 balloon animal

 magic wand

 broom

 guitar

 magnifying glass

 cowboy hat

 flippers

 fake ears

 watering can

 jack-o'-lantern

 glove

31

FOUND EVERYTHING?

Not quite! Flip Back and see if you can find these sneaky items.

school bus

blimp

peacock

31
number

windmill

can of worms

lamb

kangaroo

swan

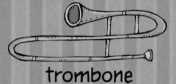
trombone

rubber duck

red sock

magnet

watch

owl

light bulb

broom